PORTRAITS:

Wooden Houses of Key West

William H. Albury House   730 Southard Street

PORTRAITS:
Wooden Houses of Key West

Commentary by
Sharon Wells, Project Director

Photographs by
Lawson Little

Includes
Old Island Restoration Commission's
Architectural Guidelines

Published by
Historic Key West Preservation Board
Florida Department of State
1982

The research and photographic work for this book was supported by a grant from the Heritage Conservation and Recreation Service, U.S. Department of the Interior, through the Florida Division of Archives, History & Records Management, Department of State, Tallahassee, Florida.

Our special thanks to Wright Langley, Betty Bruce, Nan Mirzaoff, Tom Pope, and Ann Irvine for their support and encouragement.

Technical Note: All large format architectural views were taken by an 8 x 10 view camera with a 165 mm f/8 Schneider Super Angulon lens. Plus-X sheet film was processed in either HC-110 or D-76 1:1. Most images were exposed at f/64 for from five to 90 seconds. Architectural details were photographed with a Pentax 6 x 7 and a 55 mm f/3.5 wide angle lens. Tri-X film was developed in D-23.

Design by Susie Latham and Sharon Wells
Layout by Susie Latham
Typeset in Goudy Old Style by Supertype, Inc., Hialeah, Florida.

Published in the United States by
The Historic Key West Preservation Board,
500 Whitehead Street, Key West, Florida 33040

CONTENTS

AUTHORS' NOTE

This volume of photographs focusing upon contemporary architectural images of Key West evolved from a desire to document a rapidly changing environment. Nowhere else in Florida does such a grand and magnificent display of nineteenth century wood frame structures survive. Few other cities in America can claim such a collection of Victorian houses. These photographic images represent an exploration into the basic simplicity and virtual timelessness of architectural forms in Key West. They impart, too, a sense of diversity within building styles typified by common features.

Over the past decade a significant number of these antique wooden edifices has been razed, destroyed or damaged. Essentially, they have vanished — to exist only in the realms of memory or photographic record. Many other structures have been altered greatly beyond their original appearance. These, too, are difficult to recall exactly as they once were. The distinguishing features and singular details of extant structures, which together create that special ambiance intrinsic to Key West's vernacular architecture, are captured here in the form of latent images. From mansions to cottages — each is decked with a pristine splendor that sets it apart; and all are contributory to the stately, wooden elegance amidst the tropics.

The authors envision their collaborative effort as a significant step towards the preservation of Key West's island architecture. Through personal interpretations, we have attempted to convey the sense of each dwelling as part of the fabric of the island city.

To communicate the *feeling* of a building as well as its physical appearance is our aim.

To photograph these treasures of a seaport town so that their surviving heritage will be preserved is our hope.

To document the architecture and to create art within each document is our purpose.

426 Elizabeth Street   701 & 703 Fleming Street

PREFACE

Key West, outermost link of Florida's southern archipelago, retains an architectural legacy that is unique. Isolated from the mainland and approached solely by sea until the advent of the railroad in 1912, Key West is an island dotted with residences of frame, weathered by time and tropics, which maintain an elegant simplicity of design. Starkly they rise — most are glistening white or pastel-shaded structures; others remain unpainted, testaments to an earlier time...

Former dwellings of Cuban cigarmakers and spongers, clapboarded, narrow and shuttered, stand juxtaposed to more stately classic revival homes. All are distinctive and often individualized by the wooden tracery of gingerbread. Hand-cut balustrades stretch between upstanding pillars—each exhibits a decorative incised pattern that has become a personal signature of the Victorian Age. Balustrades and balconies, trimmed with scrollwork and flourishes etched from wood by skilled carpenters, adorn and particularize the facades of Conch structures. Houses are perched upon piers, with gabled roofs that cut geometric shapes into the skyline. Edifices which, with their open porches and encircling verandas, recall an earlier era when spongers and wreckers, turtlers and cigarmakers prevailed.

This grand collection of nineteenth century residences in Key West is a visual feast. Collectively, they impart a contemporary vision of an antique landscape — one to be celebrated and preserved.

Jefferson Adams House   *804 Caroline Street*

A PATCHWORK ARCHITECTURE

Key West's treasury of handcrafted wooden houses comprises no simple, pure style. Rather, the collection forms an eclectic architecture that draws upon a legacy of Bahamian, New England, Creole and Victorian influences. What emerges from this mélange is an indigenous architecture, adapted to the tropics and inspired by carpenters whose early mastery was shipbuilding.

Gabled mansions with towers sit adjacent to smaller classic revival cottages; beautiful old Victorians with bay windows neighbor delightfully ramshackle shotguns; neatly dormered bungalows border more imposing eyebrow houses. From shacks to more palatial residences, Key West's dwellings embody a patchwork architecture — age-old weathered constructions that retain a present-day freshness and vitality of spirit.

Each house is a portrait unto itself.

BAHAMIAN INFLUENCES

The Bahama Islands comprise a chain that stretches for nearly 600 miles in the tropics off the coast of Florida. There the earliest settlers sustained a livelihood totally dependent upon the sea. During the seventeenth century small maritime stations flourished on the islands. To this original West Indian population, traditionally called Conchs (from their predilection for the shellfish *Strombus gigas,* or conch), were added seafaring English adventurers. For a time the Bahamas remained thinly populated – a base for piracy and privateering, a wrecker's haven. The American Revolution sparked an influx to the islands of several thousand displaced loyalists, or Tories, from Georgia, the Carolinas, Virginia and New York. The population trebled between 1783 and 1788; Nassau and Green Turtle Key emerged as principal settlements and ports.

For the islanders life centered around the encircling waters – from it they garnered fish, turtles and sponges. Shipbuilding skills were honed and sharpened to a level of mastery that produced rugged well-crafted schooners, sloops and square-rigged vessels that explored the Florida Keys and the Caribbean. The mariners' proficiency of design and accomplishments at wooden construction carried over from sea to land. Shipbuilders became carpenter-architects on shore. They used no formal sets of plans, yet produced a distinctive and functional architecture refined from their practical experience at precise, durable ship construction.

Inspired by recollections of New England seacoast architecture as well as their native techniques and concepts, Bahamian carpenters fashioned a simple vernacular building style – a forerunner to the remarkable nineteenth century Key West frameworks.

Certain features of Key West's carpenter-built structures, commonly called Conch architecture, were derived directly from the Bahamas. Two homes, one owned by John Bartlum and the other by Richard Roberts, were disassembled from their original sites on Green Turtle Cay and transported to Key West by ship where they were reconstructed in 1847. Both residences, the Bartlum House at 730 Eaton Street and the Roberts House at 408 William Street, are classic examples of Bahamian homes built by expert carpenter-shipbuilders. The building material was wood: yellow or white pine from Pensacola and other ports, mahogany, cypress or juniper from the Upper Keys, cedar from Cedar Key.

Richard Roberts House   *408 William Street*

The braced frame construction was characterized by mortise and tenon joinery. By this method timbers were notched to fit within each other and fastened together with long wooden pegs rather than nails. Other distinguishing elements include: a two-story edifice with an exterior staircase, spacious verandas that wrap around the house, a simple balustrade, shuttered doorways and windows, and a gable roof, originally covered by cedar or cypress shingles. A unique lapsiding of wide, flat boards, often with a beaded edge, covered the exterior. Clapboards, or weatherboards, also provided sheathing. Bahama houses were elevated on wood or stone piers to capture the prevailing winds and to prevent flood or hurricane damage.

A hall and parlor plan typified the interior arrangement of rooms. The narrow hallway was reminiscent of one on board ship. Interior walls were generally random width boards; ceilings were low with exposed beams. Graceful, hand-chiseled moldings around the entries and windows provided the sole decorative elements in the unpretentious residence of a mariner. Kitchens were simple, detached buildings with a chimney. Both the cookhouse and outhouse were located to the rear of the house. Another Bahamian carry-over, the cistern, was built of brick or masonry. Such a tank would collect fresh water for storage as it funneled through gutters and downspouts from the roof.

Thus, a wooden architecture bred in the Bahamian tropics was transplanted to Key West. It took root just as the tiny island began its transition from an isolated wrecking depot to a seaport community of nearly 2,000 by 1850. Mariners and merchants, sailors and salvors, wreckers, auctioneers and wharf owners – these early Key Westers witnessed the establishment of the town as a port of entry and the site of a district admiralty court. Wrecking, always a chancey business, brought a new lucrativeness to the island city by the 1860's. Patrician residences of the wealthy arose; stately, elegant and balconied homes with a Bahamian flavor. Such buildings are lasting tributes to shipbuilding craftsmanship.

John Lowe, Jr. House   *620 Southard Street*

George Carey House   410 Caroline Street

VARIATIONS OF A CLASSIC THEME

Gracious, distinctive examples of Classic Revival architecture stand parade-like along the streets and lanes of old Key West. The prolific display of century-old houses, some dilapidated by age and others refreshed by a coat of new paint, are eloquent manifestations of the era of Romanticism in America. Monuments to classicism, these Conch houses embody a simplicity and sense of proportion derived directly from Greek and Roman forms. Adaptations of the Greek temple facade together with architectural elements such as pedimented gables, columns, corner pilasters and cornices closely identify the style. Such classic forms originated with the ancients, were adopted in England and transplanted to New England and grace Key West's island landscape to this day.

Classically inspired architecture first appeared in the United States in the 1820's. Handcrafted, weatherboarded Key West residences echo those built during the clipper ship days in New England. Typically unelaborate, yet formal in appearance, the island's Revival homes represent variations on a classic theme.

Most abundant are those side-hall plan buildings in which the gable forms the main front of the house. The facade is crowned with a classic pediment; plain or chamfered wooden posts function as columns. The two-storied vertical demeanor is capped by a high-peaked tin roof that shines with a silver luminescence. A second variation in style is represented by those houses where a pedimented gable dominates the facade, but does not include the main entrance. Two-story balconies parallel the street and often an exterior staircase is visible. A central hall plan is typical. Porches and balconies are enclosed by carved balustrades and lend a dignity to the design. Thirdly, the "eyebrow" style house is a bit of domestic architecture unique to Key West. It is characterized by a series of "eyebrow" windows set beneath a heavy roof overhang. Porch posts rise starkly from the floor to the roof eave. Finally, there exist smaller, classically inspired wooden houses that retain a simple charm. These one-story residences have a recessed apron porch and trace their lineage to Creole cottages of the Louisiana bayou region.

These four architectural forms typify Classic Revival structures in Key West. Varied geographic influences have intermingled to produce an architecture indigenous to island life. Many other buildings are difficult to categorize, yet retain certain classic allusions: a harmonious scale and proportion, details reminiscent of Greek orders, rectangular transsoms over doorways, simple moldings, the ubiquitous porches and balconies.

The Victorian Age witnessed the introduction of the scroll saw and turning lathe for carpenter-architects. Wooden filigree, called gingerbread, added whimsical decorations and patterns to each framework. Chiselled details, jigcut and spindle balusters, carved corner brackets, wooden trimwork — all bestowed a lace-like icing to the gingerbread houses. Such embellishments became signatures of the Victorian Age.

The stately, yet unpretentious dwellings of classic design remain enduring sights in Key West.

Edward Roberts House   *643 William Street*

John T. Sawyer House   609 *Frances Street*

Frederick Filer House   *724 Eaton Street*

709 Olivia Street

Benjamin P. Baker House   615 Elizabeth Street

820 Georgia Street

Randall Adams/John H. Roberts House   *701 Southard Street*

J. Vining Harris House   1401 Duval Street

QUEEN ANNE ARCHITECTURE

The inventiveness of Key West's carpenter-architects is apparent in the exuberant splashes of Queen Anne architecture that arose in the last quarter of the nineteenth century. Begun in England in the 1860's, it became popular between the years 1876 and 1910, Key West's heyday. The island was booming; it was the most populated and wealthiest Florida city. Improvisations upon the grandness of the formal Queen Anne style adapted easily to the tropical setting. Elegance and whimsy, particularized by abundant gingerbread tracery, touched these antique dwellings in the Victorian era.

Variety is the hallmark of Queen Anne architecture. These houses are characterized by a deliberate complexity and generally follow an asymmetrical or rambling plan. Ideally, each facade is different in height and appearance and may display a multitude of shapes, colors and textures. Attached towers or turrets, projecting bays, ornamented gables, balconies or porches decked with wooden filigree, dormers, bargeboards and a richness of exterior decorative trim denote a Queen Anne structure. Such a mélange of patterns and details have contributed a fancifulness to the island landscape.

In Key West the ensemble of late Victorian buildings that exhibit Queen Anne characteristics include: the J.V. Harris brick residence (the Southernmost House), the Elks Club on Duval Street, and a number of wood frame houses such as those at 313 William Street and 1017 Southard Street. A few small Queen Anne cottages, each with a cross gable roof, are also to be discovered on the island.

810 Eisenhower Drive

George Bowne Patterson House   *522 Caroline Street*

615 Fleming Street
A detail of balusters and gingerbread

508 Simonton Street
Spindle stringcourse and corner brackets typify gingerbread decoration

602 Southard Street
Elaborate brackets on Mason S. Moreno House

Jigcut corner brackets with sculpted column

George A. Roberts House   313 William Street

E.H. Gato, Jr. House   *1327 Duval Street*

829 Emma Street

THE CIGARMAKING ERA

Key West's rise to industrial prominence was a direct outgrowth of the Ten Years War in Cuba. That civil strife heralded massive population shifts in the late 1860's. By the end of the first year of armed struggle, 100,000 Cubans had sought refuge abroad. The decade of the 1880's saw the arrival of thousands of Cuban emigres seeking relief from the repressive martial law that had enveloped the revolution-torn nation. Concomitantly, resourceful Havana cigar manufacturers relocated their operations to the United States; Key West became a prime site. The southernmost city afforded easy access to both the Cuban tobacco regions and the commercial market of Havana. The island's labor force, greatly expanding to include the influx of migratory Cuban workers, supported the burgeoning industry as well.

Cigar manufacturing had its beginnings as early as 1831 and had reached its zenith by 1890. Factories and warehouses sprang up in various sectors of the city, employing strippers, trimmers, pickers and packers by the thousands. The industry mushroomed so quickly that by 1880 there were 57 major manufacturers who employed from five to five hundred laborers. In 1883 eighty cigar factories engaged 2,700 operatives in the production of 42 million hand-rolled cigars. Five years later 166 factories were producing nearly 100 million cigars in the island city. The Cortez Company and the factories of Eduardo H. Gato, Vicente Martinez Ybor, Francisco Marrero, H.R. Kelly and William Seidenberg figured as Key West's most significant tobacco conglomerates. Although the decline and fall of the cigar empire in Key West began as the twentieth century opened, tangible traces of its existence endure. Sole remnants of a vanished past, cigarmakers' cottages still stand as witnesses to a time when Key West emerged as the major cigar manufacturing center in America.

SHOTGUN HOUSES

The decade between 1880 and 1890 witnessed the greatest building surge in Key West's history. Cigar entrepreneurs erected dozens of factories of substantial size to house the shipping departments, casing quarters and packing rooms for the cigar workers. Often the owners would buy blocks of nearby property on which to build dwellings for their employees. Such houses were characterized by balloon frame construction and a shotgun-style configuration.

Tracing its roots to West Africa and the French Caribbean, the shotgun plan of architecture was transported to the United States and relocated particularly in the southern Gulf Coast region. From there indigenous adaptations evolved.

In Key West each of these single story, one-room wide buildings usually incorporates a side hall plan with three rooms, one behind the other. Variations of this simple design, of course, exist. A shotgun structure sits with its roof ridge perpendicular to the street and its front door on the gable end. Generally, a two or three bay porch, incised or attached, lines the facade; a simple slat balustrade may also be found. Most often, the pillars are plain square posts, unadorned by capitals or sculpted elements. A few shotguns exhibit turned posts and scrolled corner brackets.

Shotgun dwellings reflect additional characterizing elements. Windows on these wooden cottages, like most other Conch houses, are nearly always shuttered to filter the heat and bright sunlight. Traditionally, the window sashes contain either two or six lights in each sash, and thus are termed 2/2 or 6/6 double hung sash types. Roof openings, called scuttles, provide increased air circulation. Tacked-on additions behind the main building create a roofline that cuts sharp-edged designs into the sky. In past times, outdoor privies were located to the rear of the house. More often than not, the small yards were outlined by picket fences that were either whitewashed or left unpainted.

By 1883, more than 8,000 cigar workers required housing in Key West. This fact was instrumental in spurring a turn-of-the-century building impetus. Although hastily erected to satisfy this immediate housing demand, these wooden shotgun dwellings reflected the same durable construction techniques and materials that characterized the more munificent Victorian residences. And they have persisted, well-loved by their inhabitants, for nearly a century.

1007 Fleming Street

Fernando W. Roberts' cigarmakers' cottages   822-830 Olivia Street

516 Bahama Street

1127 United Street

Solares Hill, corner of Elizabeth and Angela Streets

FRAME VERNACULAR HOUSES

The hundreds of frame houses in Key West, each with its own personality, comprise a living museum of antiquity. Clearly indigenous to the tropical spirit, the handsome wooden homes retain the special patina of age. Many of the structures fall into no formal category of style and are generally classed as frame vernacular dwellings.

These vernacular exhibits of architecture manifest a plain facade with shuttered openings and lack stylistic or decorative details. Most are one and a half stories, rectangular in plan with a gable roof. Roof hatches called scuttles are often evident on these as well as other Key West homes. The simple flat facade is proportioned into three bays by square pillars. A balustraded porch covered by a shed roof may wrap around more than a single side. Neither entablatures nor pediments over windows and doorways are evident. Although not as elaborate as classic revivals or Queen Anne houses, these vernacular buildings maintain construction techniques and building materials consistent with the existing ensemble of Conch architecture.

Key West's carpenter-built architecture persisted despite severe hurricanes in 1846, 1909, and 1910 and the disastrous fire of 1886, which swept from the San Carlos Hall on Duval Street northward to the wharves and docks at the Gulf's edge. Key West, a town built entirely of wood, lay scorched, ravished by flames. Whole blocks were razed. The island was left a tropical wasteland.

Yet the destruction and havoc wreaked upon the city lasted for only a brief period. Skilled carpenters and craftsmen began immediately to rebuild the community. Balloon frames arose, replacing the post and beam construction forms. Cut and wire nails rather than wooden pegs, or trenails, fastened the timbers; the exterior was clapboarded. Houses were ground pinned, or anchored to the native rock. Within a short time factories, stores, sponge houses and residences were reconstructed with precision.

905 Angela Street

1025 Varela Street

Gideon Lowe House   *409 William Street*

Gideon Lowe House   *409 William Street*

INTERIOR SPACES

Conch house interiors recall a time and place of the past. Some survive virtually intact; high ceilings that create an openness, spacious rooms that display a marvelous array of fine detailing and woodwork. Beautifully crafted staircases with sculptured balusters and carved newel posts lend a classic quality to many homes. Simpler houses, too, are no less reflective of authentic details. Each is truly distinctive.

Many house interiors have been altered, modernized or allowed to deteriorate, thus concealing or losing much of their early identity. For the restoration enthusiast, traces of original elements such as wainscotting, wallpaper, stencilled designs, moldings and cornices may still be discernible. Careful examination of paint chips and nails or wooden pegs may provide additional clues to the original structure.

Photographs of entrance halls, staircases and several distinctive rooms of three Key West residences were selected to illustrate distinguished restoration efforts.

823 Eaton Street

Gideon Lowe House   409 William Street

823 Eaton Street

Benjamin D. Trevor House   1311 Truman Avenue

Benjamin D. Trevor House   1311 Truman Avenue

Richard Peacon House   *712 Eaton Street*

TO PRESERVE AND RESTORE...

Time has touched the elegant structures; some have been carelessly neglected, others abandoned and still others maintained with love and affection. Many remain essentially unchanged from an early era. Parts of yesterday's Key West have vanished and other portions are rapidly disappearing. For decades the architecture of Key West has been largely overlooked.

In light of the emerging national interest in historic preservation and restoration, people in Key West are realizing that one of their most irreplaceable cultural resources is the collection of antique wooden dwellings called Conch Houses. To preserve that special character and inheritance of the built environment is imperative. The richness of texture, the simplicity of design, as well as the intimate scale of houses that sit row after row on narrow streets, lend themselves to a visual appreciation that is special.

A truly effective program of restoration, initiated and carried forth by caring individuals could push Key West to center stage in the preservation arena.

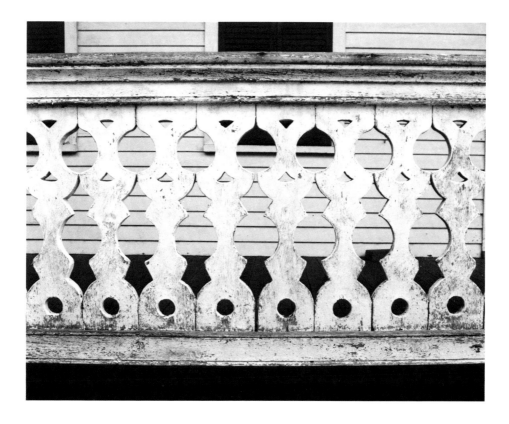

528 Simonton Street
Mirador atop John B. Maloney House / B'nai Brith Synagogue

PRESERVATION GUIDELINES

The Old Island Restoration Commission (OIRC) serves as the architectural review board for the HP-1, HP-2 zones and the historic district of the City of Key West. City Ordinance 69-1187 states that application by the house owner for a permit . . . must be made to OIRC, "accompanied by full plans and specifications . . ., so far as they relate to the proposed appearance, color, texture or materials and architectural design of the *exterior,* including the front, sides, rear and roof of a building, alterations or addition of any outbuildings, party wall, courtyard, fence or other dependency thereof . . ."

Forms for application to OIRC are available at the City Building Department. The Commission meets every second and fourth Monday of the month at 5:00 p.m. in the City Commission Chamber at City Hall. The completed application, plans and photographs should be submitted to the City Building Department for review prior to the next board meeting.

In support of the work of the Old Island Restoration Commission, the Historic Key West Preservation Board is including the OIRC guidelines for renovation and restoration. These architectural guidelines describe items and materials traditional to Key West architecture. They serve as guides for the owner in the repair and preservation of his building.

HISTORICAL RESOURCE PROTECTION

The following criteria shall be utilized as guidelines in conjunction with Key West Ordinance No. 69-29, Sections XIII, XIV and XV by the Board of Adjustment when a certificate of appropriateness, special exception or variance is required. The following criteria shall be utilized by the Old Island Restoration Commission in formulating their recommendations to approve, deny or modify permits for improvements, alterations, reconstruction, restoration and new construction in the Key West Historical District. The guidelines shall apply only to buildings and portions thereof that are visible from a public way.

OIRC ARCHITECTURAL GUIDELINES

EXTERIOR RENOVATION

EXTERIOR SIDING

For exterior horizontal siding, weather boards or clapboards, ½″ x 6″ are recommended. Both vertical siding or board and batten siding are acceptable. Wide beaded-edge siding is a unique factor of the District, and thus acceptable. In no case should plywood, metal, stucco, brick veneer over wood, or any imitative material be used for restoration. Although there is very little masonry construction within the residential areas, it is acceptable with certain limitations. Concrete block, glass blocks, heavily stuccoed exteriors or brick in any of the wide variety of contemporary colors, such as salmon, buff, yellow shall be unacceptable.

526 Frances Street

ROOFING

For roofing materials, metal shingles are recommended. If these are not available, use V-crimp metal roofing. Fire resistant asphalt or asbestos shingles of rectangular design, 325 lb. minimum weight, in white or gray are acceptable. Wood shingles are acceptable as a roof covering, but not for exterior siding. Most favored material, where possible, would be fire-retardant cedar or cypress shakes.

WINDOWS

Windows and their surrounding elements establish the basic character of many buildings. Therefore, the greatest care should be taken when replacing or remodeling these items. Window surrounds are generally plain with little ornamentation. Wooden drip molds characterize the vast majority of structures although pediments over the windows and entries are often found on the more elaborate Conch houses.

Window types that are historically correct and most appropriate to Key West houses are double hung sash windows: "one-over-one," "two-over-two," and "six-over-six," referring to the number of subdivisions in each moving sash. Care should be taken to maintain the vertical effect of panes when replacing double hung sash windows.

For window frames and sashes wood is the recommended replacement material. If aluminum windows rather than the traditional wooden framed double hung sash windows are used for replacements, they should have a factory applied white or corresponding trim color finish. Mill finish is not acceptable.

SHUTTERS

Historically, Key West residences and buildings have always exhibited wooden shutters of various types at doorways and windows. Shutters allow air to circulate through the house while screening out the heat and bright sunlight. Both movable and fixed louvers, top-mounted sun screen shutters, solid vertical slat shutters and shutters with screens are all acceptable types indigenous to the tropical climate of the island. Wood is the required material for replacement of shutters.

FENCES

Wooden picket fences are contributory to the rhythmic frameworks of Key West neighborhoods. In the 1820's, vertical planks or palings were erected around the earliest frame cottages. Later nineteenth century photographs reveal that most island residences were outlined by pickets – sometimes painted white, more often whitewashed or left unpainted. Fences in the city display a multitude of forms – square vertical planks, rounded wood pegs, narrow boards with incised designs or scalloped edges – all continue the wooden aspect of Conch architecture, with each one lending its own distinctive charm to the residence it encloses.

Regulations for erection of fences in the residential and commercial historic area require (1) four foot high solid or open fences or (2) six foot high fences on the side and rear property lines if the upper two feet contain 50% openings of repeated patterns. The scale of the fence and especially of its posts and gates should be in keeping with the house and exhibit compatibility with the neighborhood architecture.

Wood, wrought iron or cast iron are the recommended materials traditional to Old Town Key West. Masonry is acceptable, providing the upper portions use wood balusters or iron fencing.

Chain link fencing does NOT contribute visually to an historic district.

ENTRANCES, DOORWAYS & PORCHES

The doorway is one of the main indicators of the character of a building. Every effort should be made to maintain the basic symmetry and vertical proportions of the doorway. Original features such as sidelights, fan lights, transoms, molded and panelled doors (often with glass in the upper panels) and exterior molding details should be retained in a renovation. Removing entryway features often destroys the symmetry and balance intended by the builder.

Wood is the recommended replacement material for doors, screen doors, porches, railings and steps.

Tongue and groove construction of porch flooring is historically correct.

GINGERBREAD & DECORATIVE ELEMENTS

Original wooden ornamentation, balusters (machine-turned spindles and jig-cut posts) balustrade rails, corner brackets, dentils, and umbricated shingles should be saved where possible. Original materials and motifs should be duplicated during restoration. Historical photographs and research can help substantiate the existence and style of any original decorative elements.

PAINT COLORS

Key West is a showcase of an indigenous style of Victorian architecture, one permeated by a Caribbean influence. Historically, most Conch houses were either painted white with a dark green trim or remained unpainted. In more recent years, tropical colors traditional to the Caribbean Islands have particularized the residences and maintain the spirit of the island architecture.

The colorful individual buildings have great value, but in a larger sense it is the relation of one building to another, the grouping and contrasting of structures along a street and the contrast of one street to another, that creates in the visitor's mind the true image of distinctive character. The city can be regarded as a living museum when the people truly act as curators.

ACCEPTABLE PAINT COLORS

Acceptable paint colors for the historic district are white, light gray or pastel shades with corresponding trim color.

525 Simonton Street   *Classic arched pediment over doorway*

SITING

No existent building shall be relocated and no new structure shall be placed closer to the sidewalk, street or visible alley, than that distance which has been predetermined by existent historic structures. Areas which have traditionally been reserved for parks and open spaces should remain as such. Criteria for building setback will be established either by studying original zoning permits and plat maps or by establishing uniform setback.

SCALE

No existent historic building shall be enlarged and no new structure shall be built so that its proportions, particularly height, are out of scale with its surroundings. On any given block or area where a variety of sizes and styles exist, no structure, either new or enlarged, shall outsize the majority of the structures in that area. If it is mandatory for any of a number of reasons that a private dwelling be enlarged, these alterations shall be made in such a manner as not to alter the scale of the streetscape. The height of all new construction shall be based upon the height of existing structures within the vicinity and generally shall not exceed a maximum height of two and one-half (2½) stories.

Balcony of Charles J. Curtis House   603 Southard Street

NATIONAL REGISTER OF HISTORIC PLACES

The National Register of Historic Places is the official list of the Nation's cultural resources worthy of preservation. Historic sites listed or eligible for listing on the National Register enjoy special tax and funding advantages under several state and federal programs. Owners who rehabilitate certified historic properties are eligible for Federal tax benefits. All sites enumerated on the National Register, regardless of type of ownership, are automatically eligible for federal matching grants-in-aid for acquisition or restoration purposes. Sites considered eligible for the National Register, as well as sites already listed, are given priority consideration in the granting of H.U.D. Community Development Block Grants, FHA Title I insured loans, and other forms of federal financial assistance. Listing on the National Register provides protection by requiring comment from the Advisory Council on Historic Preservation on the effect of federally assisted projects on the resources.

The National Register includes historic districts, sites, buildings, structures and objects of significance in American history, architecture, archeology and culture. In 1971 a significant area of the Old Town Section of the City of Key West was placed on the National Register. Currently, in 1982, efforts are under way to expand Key West's National Historic District boundaries to more than double the original area and to embrace Duval Street from the waters of the Gulf to the Atlantic.

Nine Key West buildings are individually listed on the National Register. They include: The E.H. Gato House, The Joseph Yates Porter House, The Tift-Hemingway House, East Martello Tower, The Customs House/Post Office, Fort Zachary Taylor, The National Guard Armory, Coast Guard Building #1 and the Little White House.

John Weech House   *1217 White Street*

THE AUTHORS

Sharon Wells, Historian for the Historic Key West Preservation Board since 1978, received a B.A. with Honors in History from the University of Florida. Ms. Wells worked for three years as survey historian and photographer for the Division of Archives, History & Records Management in Tallahassee, Florida. She is the author of numerous studies: *The Oldest House: An Historical Record* and *Naval Architecture of Key West: A Survey of Historic Structures at Truman Annex*. In 1982 her publications included: *Forgotten Legacy: Blacks in Nineteenth Century* and *Key West: Illuminations of an Island.*

Lawson Little received a B.F.A. from Rhode Island School of Design where he studied under Harry Callahan. Mr. Little is instructor of photography at Florida Keys Community College and co-author of *Same Train. Different Time.*, a photographic study on American railroad steam engineers. He is s 1979 recipient of a Florida Fine Arts Council grant. Little's work is included in collections at the Museum of Modern Art, Art Institute of Chicago and the George Eastman House, Rochester, New York.

SELECTED SOURCES

Books

Benjamin, Asher. *The American Builder's Companion.* Reprint of the 6th (1827) edition. New York: Dover Pub., 1969.

Bicknell, A.J. & W.T. Comstock. *Victorian Architecture: Two Pattern Books (1873 and 1881).* New York: American Life Foundation, 1975.

Browne, Jefferson B. *Key West: The Old and the New.* Reprint of 1912 edition. Gainesville: University of Florida Press, 1976.

Bullock, Orin M., Jr. *The Restoration Manual.* Norwalk: Selvermine Press, 1966.

Cultural Resource Survey of Key West. Miscellaneous Project Report Series No. 48. Tallahassee: Division of Archives, History & Records Management, Department of State, 1979.

Federal Writers' Project (WPA). *A Guide to Key West.* Hastings House, 1949.

Langley, Wright and Stan Windhorn. *Yesterday's Key West.* Miami: E.A. Seemann Publishing, Inc., 1973.

Old Island Restoration Commission. *Preservation Guidebook for the Old Section.* Key West, 1975.

Olwell, Carol and Judith Waldhorn. *A Gift To The Street.* San Francisco: Antelope Press, 1976.

Sherrill, Chris and Roger Aiello. *Key West: The Last Resort.* Key West: Key West Book and Card Company, 1978.

Standards for Rehabilitation and Guidelines for Rehabilitating Historic Buildings. Office of Archeology and Historic Preservation, Heritage Conservation and Recreation Service, U.S. Department of the Interior.

Stephen, George. *Remodeling Old Houses Without Destroying Their Character.* New York: Alfred A. Knopf, 1973.

Wiffen, Marcus. *American Architecture Since 1780: A Guide to the Styles.* Cambridge, Mass.: MIT Press, 1969.

Periodicals

American Preservation. P.O. Box 2451, Little Rock, Arkansas 72203. Excellent bi-monthly magazine on historic preservation.

Historic Preservation & Preservation News. Washington, D.C.: The Preservation Press.

The Old-House Journal. Brooklyn, N.Y.; The Old-House Journal Company. Excellent source which addresses renovation and maintenance techniques for older houses.